Smithsonian

OCEAN DISCOVERIES

by TAMRA B. ORR

Raintree is an imprint of Capstone Global Library Limited, a company incorporated in England and Wales having its registered office at 264 Banbury Road, Oxford, OX2 7DY – Registered company number: 6695582

www.raintree.co.uk
myorders@raintree.co.uk

Edited by Michelle Hasselius
Designed by Heidi Thompson
Original illustrations © Capstone Global Library Limited 2019
Picture research by Svetlana Zhurkin
Production by Kris Wilfahrt
Originated by Capstone Global Library Ltd
Printed and bound in India

ISBN 978 1 4747 5970 0
22 21 20 19 18
10 9 8 7 6 5 4 3 2 1

British Library Cataloguing in Publication Data
A full catalogue record for this book is available from the British Library.

Our very special thanks to Don E. Wilson, Curator Emeritus, Vertebrate Zoology at the National Museum of Natural History, for his review. Capstone would also like to thank the following at Smithsonian Enterprises: Kealy Gordon, Product Development Manag... ... Manager;
Brigid Ferraro, Vice Presiden... ...Consumer Products; and
Carol LeBlanc, Senior Vice Pr... ...on and Consumer Products.

Acknowledgements
We would like to thank the following for permission to reproduce photographs: © Greenpeace, 12; Alamy: Helmut Corneli, 5; Courtesy of Laura E. Bagge, 14; Getty Images: Dante Fenolio, 23, Franco Banfi, 10; Greg Rouse, 9; MBARI: © 2006, 20, © 2009 Todd Walsh, 21 (right), © 2012, 21 (left); Minden Pictures: Solvin Zankl, cover (bottom), 15; NASA: JPL, 29 (left), JPL/Space Science Institute, 29 (right), JPL-Caltech, 28; Nature Picture Library: David Shale, 26; Newscom: Polaris/Tasso Taraboulsi, 7; NOAA Ocean Explorer, 22; Scripps Institution of Oceanography at UC San Diego: Emily Kelly, 19; Shutterstock: Alexander Kolomietz, 16, Damsea, 27, David Litman, 8, divedog, cover (top), JC Photo, 13, JonMilnes, 4, Olga Khoroshunova, 25, Peter Hermes Furian, 6, pingebat (coral), 1 and throughout, Russ Heinl, 17, Volina, 24 (right), Wildnerdpix, 24 (left)

Quote Sources
Page 7, "'Faceless' Fish Missing for More Than a Century Rediscovered by Australian Scientists." 31 May 2017. The Guardian. https://www.theguardian.com/environment/2017/may/31/faceless-fish-missing-for-more-than-a-century-rediscovered-by-australian-scientists

Page 14, "This Ocean Creature Makes Its Own Invisibility Cloak." 9 December 2016. National Geographic. https://news.nationalgeographic.com/2016/12/oceans-animals-invisible-physics/

Page 17, "How Drones Can Help Leopard Seals." 19 December 2017. Discover Wildlife. http://www.discoverwildlife.com/news/how-drones-can-help-leopard-seals

Page 29, "NASA Missions Provide New Insights into 'Ocean Worlds' in Our Solar System." 12 April 2017. NASA. https://www.nasa.gov/press-release/nasa-missions-provide-new-insights-into-ocean-worlds-in-our-solar-system

CONTENTS

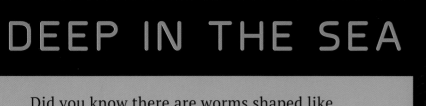

Did you know there are worms shaped like Christmas trees living in the Great Barrier Reef? Have you heard of the anglerfish? It has a glowing light above its mouth. Creatures living under the ocean's surface are fascinating and mysterious – and those are just the ones scientists know about.

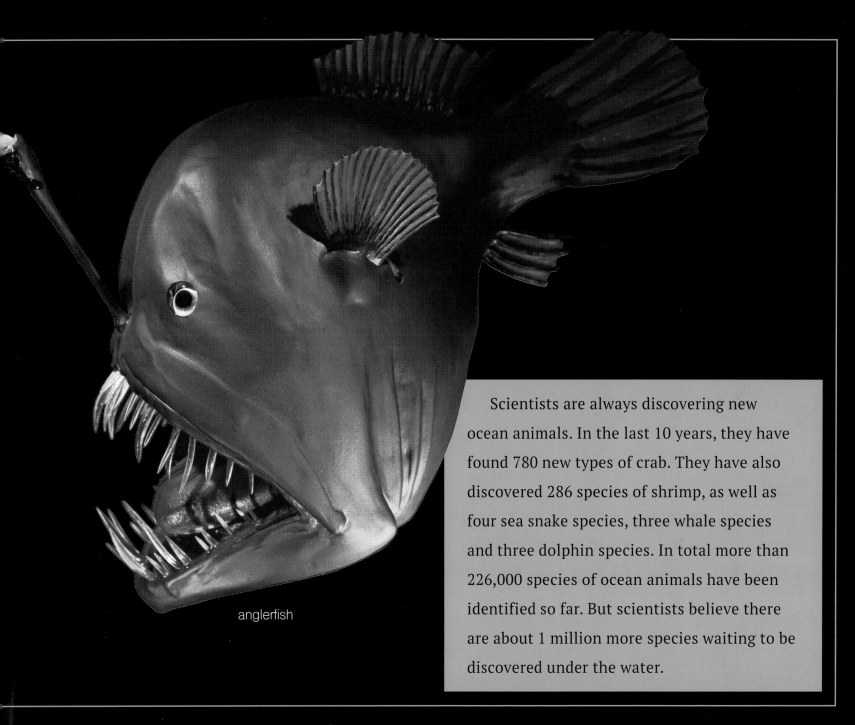

anglerfish

Scientists are always discovering new ocean animals. In the last 10 years, they have found 780 new types of crab. They have also discovered 286 species of shrimp, as well as four sea snake species, three whale species and three dolphin species. In total more than 226,000 species of ocean animals have been identified so far. But scientists believe there are about 1 million more species waiting to be discovered under the water.

FACELESS FISH

What fish looks like it's missing its eyes, nose, mouth and gills? The faceless fish! In 2017, scientists from Australia spotted the fish during their expedition in the Coral Sea. The team used fishing nets and deep-sea cameras to find the fish 3,962 metres (13,000 feet) below the surface.

The faceless fish was first spotted almost 150 years ago, but was not seen again until 2017. Because these fish live so deep in the Pacific Ocean, very few have ever been caught.

"This little fish looks amazing because the mouth is actually situated at the bottom of the animal so, when you look side-on, you can't see any eyes, you can't see any nose or gills or mouth."

Tim O'Hara, expedition leader

CRUMPLED SOCK

The *Xenoturbella* look like pink socks wiggling along the ocean floor. In 2016, scientists found four new species of these marine worms in the Pacific Ocean, near California and Mexico.

The worms have no organs, which make them look like crumpled-up socks or deflated balloons. They range in size from 2.5 to 20 centimetres (1 to 8 inches) long.

The *Xenoturbella* eat clams, oysters and scallops.

rock scallops

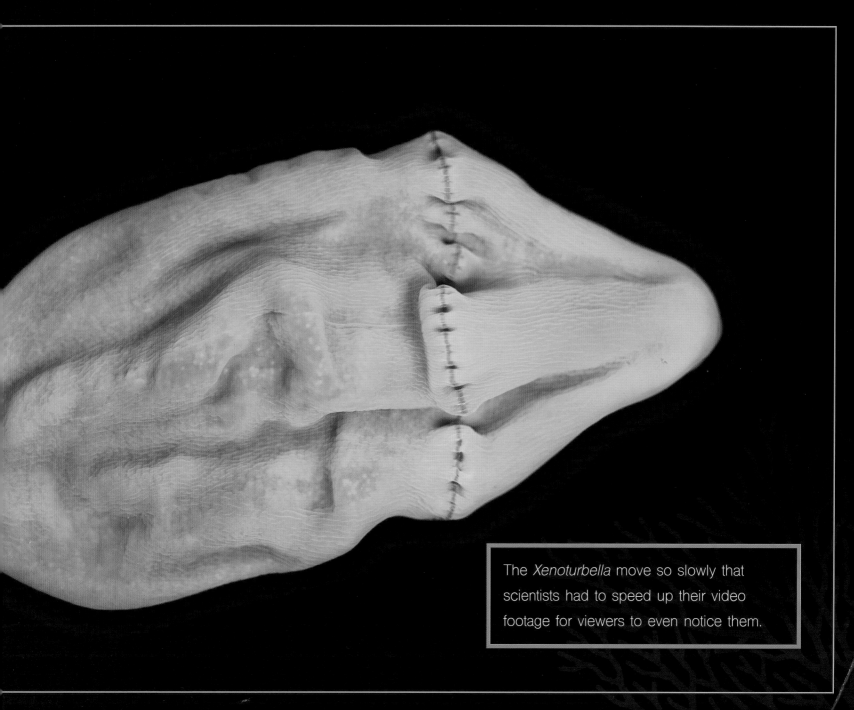

The *Xenoturbella* move so slowly that scientists had to speed up their video footage for viewers to even notice them.

A SHARK'S LIFE

The Greenland shark swims slowly in the Arctic Ocean. Scientists have known about this species since 1995. But in 2016 scientists discovered how long these sharks can live for.

Greenland sharks grow about 1.3 cm (0.5 inches) per year. Adults are 4 to 5 m (13 to 16 feet) long.

Greenland sharks do not reach adulthood until they are about 150 years old.

Because the Greenland shark has soft bones, scientists can't use them to determine the animal's age. Soft bones do not show the changes that come from aging the way that hard bones do. Instead, forensic scientists used radiocarbon dating to determine the ages of 28 Greenland sharks. The team found that one of the sharks was 400 years old. This makes the species the longest living vertebrates on Earth.

SPECIES	LIFE SPAN
geoducks	160 years
tube worms	250 years
ocean quahog	500 years

A HIDDEN CORAL REEF

It's exciting for scientists to find a new species in the ocean. Imagine finding a coral reef that's more than 960 kilometres (600 miles) long. In 2016, Brazilian and US researchers discovered a coral reef deep in the Amazon River. Most coral reefs are in shallow water to absorb the sunlight. But this reef is able to live in deeper water with limited sunlight.

Scientists found sea creatures living in the coral reef, including 61 types of sponges. One weighed more than 90 kilograms (200 pounds). That's as heavy as a baby elephant!

one of the first images of the Amazon Reef, taken from a submarine in 2017

THE GREAT BARRIER REEF

The Great Barrier Reef is the planet's largest living structure. It's so large that it can be seen from outer space! It's also at risk of dying out. Warming ocean temperatures and chemicals in the water are causing the reef to die. The Australian government is taking steps to protect the Great Barrier Reef. They are limiting what can be dumped in the water and setting up funds to protect the animals living in the reef.

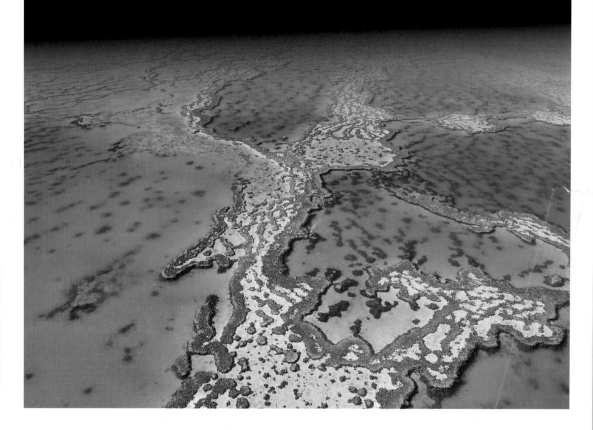

Divers are not able to study the Amazon Reef up close because of strong river currents and muddy water.

NOW YOU SEE THEM, NOW YOU DON'T

If you need to hide, making yourself invisible would certainly help. Take the hyperiid amphipod, for example. These sneaky crustaceans use an anti-reflective coating to hide from hungry predators. In 2016 Laura Bagge, a marine biologist, discovered that these species can seem invisible.

Most amphipods are not completely invisible. You can still see their colourful eyes.

"The first time we looked at what we caught, there were a whole bunch of animals in the bucket . . . I stuck my hand in the bucket . . . and instead I hit something that was hard, but I couldn't even see it . . . It looked like a glass animal."

Laura Bagge, Duke University marine biologist

Hyperiid amphipods can grow up to 18 centimetres (7 inches) long. They live in almost all of the world's oceans. They are scavengers, so they eat what they find on the ocean floor.

One of the amphipod's biggest predators are deep-sea dragon fish. Dragon fish use their own built-in lights to search for these nearly invisible creatures.

black dragon fish

KEEPING A CLOSE EYE

FROM THE SKY

Trying to track the movements and behaviours of marine animals can be difficult. They are constantly on the move, often in places that are difficult – or even dangerous – for scientists to get to. That's when it's time to call in the drones. Drones can take photos and record data quickly, without putting scientists in danger. Drones have helped with numerous projects. They have recorded coral reef changes, tracked weight changes in leopard seals and counted sea lion populations.

A hexacopter drone with a camera flies near an iceberg.

"We can get measurements that are just as good, or better, without ever bothering the animals. Catching a single seal can take hours, but the drone can photograph every seal on a beach in a few minutes."
Douglas Krause, research scientist at the Southwest Fisheries Science Centre in California

sea lions in Oregon, USA

UNDER THE WATER

Thanks to the Benthic Underwater Microscope, divers can see ocean animals up close. Researchers from Scripps Institution of Oceanography developed this underwater microscope in 2016. Scientists can study sea creatures in their natural habitats, rather than having to take them to a lab.

The Benthic Underwater Microscope has a built-in computer. It also has a ring of LED lights, a focusing lens and can turn a photo into a 3D image.

A scientist uses the Benthic Underwater Microscope to study coral.

The microscope can go 30 metres (100 feet) underwater. Most dive projects only go down 9 metres (30 feet) deep.

KILLER SPONGES

Is that innocent-looking sponge in your bathroom really a dangerous killer? No, but carnivorous sponges do live deep in the oceans. These sponges often have sharp spikes to catch prey. Between 2012 and 2014, four new species of killer sponges were found in the north-eastern Pacific Ocean. They were named by the Monterey Bay Aquarium Research Institute in California.

Some killer sponges are found near heated waters around underwater volcanoes.

One of these newly discovered sponges is the carnivorous harp sponge. It gets its name because it looks like a harp. Its branches are covered in barbed hooks and sharp spines. These sponges eat zooplankton that are pushed into the branches by the ocean's current.

Scientists use remotely operated vehicles to study sponges up close.

UNDERWATER DUMBO

The *Grimpoteuthis* is an octopus that has an extra set of rounded fins to propel itself through the ocean. The fins look like giant ears. Scientists call the tiny octopus Dumbo, after the character in the 1941 Disney film, *Dumbo*.

In 2014, a team from the National Oceanic and Atmospheric Administration captured the first video of the Dumbo octopus. The animal lives on the ocean floor, 2,990 to 3,960 metres (9,800 to 13,000 feet) underwater. It eats snails and worms.

Most Dumbo octopuses are 20 to 30 centimetres (8 to 12 inches) long. But one octopus caught in 2009 was almost 1.8 metres (6 feet) long!

Scientists have discovered more than 20 different *Grimpoteuthis* species since 1883.

UNDERWATER LANDSCAPES

   Tamu Massif is the world's largest volcano, but you'll never see it up close. That's because the volcano is more than 1.6 kilometres (1 mile) underwater. Tamu Massif was formed about 145 million years ago. It is almost 378,000 square kilometres (146,000 square miles). That's about the size of Japan.

   Oceanographer William Sager discovered the volcano in 2013, between Japan and Hawaii. He named it "tamu" after his university.

The largest active volcano on Earth is Hawaii's Mauna Loa, but it is a fraction of the size of Tamu Massif.

Mauna Loa

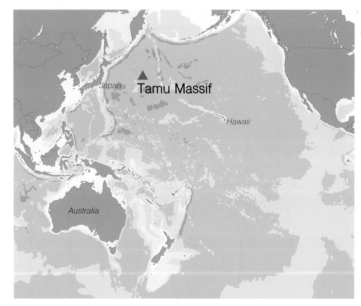

Tamu Massif

ALMOST A WATERFALL

An underwater waterfall flows just off the coast of Africa. Or does it? The waterfall is actually ocean currents pushing salt and silt from an underwater shelf to a much deeper one below. This fake waterfall is popular with tourists. They go on helicopter rides to take a closer look.

DEEP-SEA LIZARDFISH

The deep-sea lizardfish looks like a monster. It has the face of a lizard, the body of an eel and a mouth full of sharp, thin fangs. Luckily this fish is rarely seen. Researchers discovered the animal in the waters near Tasmania in 2017. The fishy predator lives 900 to 2,400 metres (3,000 to 8,000 feet) underwater. Deep-sea lizardfish will eat anything they can find, including fish, crustaceans and molluscs. They even eat each other.

THE OCEAN'S STARS

Many oceans are home to brittle stars, or ophiuroids. Brittle stars are similar to starfish. There are hundreds of species of brittle stars that come in all colours and sizes. In 2001, a new type of brittle star was found. It can change colour in order to hide from predators.

OCEANS IN OUTER SPACE

You know that there are oceans here on Earth. But did you know there are oceans in space too? Could one of these space oceans contain sea life?

In 2015, the space probe *Cassini* found hydrogen gas on one of Saturn's moons. The gas was in a large amount of icy material that sprayed up from Enceladus. Enceladus is a small moon that is covered with ice. There is a large ocean underneath the icy surface. Scientists think the gas came from the moon's ocean floor.

 ◀ *Cassini*

"This is the closest we've come, so far, to identifying a place with some of the ingredients needed for a habitable environment."

Thomas Zurbuchen, the National Aeronautics and Space Administration (NASA)

The NASA spacecraft *Cassini* was launched into space in 1997. It provided details about Saturn until 2017.

A planet needs liquid water, a source of energy and certain chemicals such as hydrogen, oxygen and carbon for life to survive. Because of this discovery, scientists know that Enceladus' ocean has some of the chemicals needed to support life. Who knows if alien sea creatures are swimming in Enceladus' ocean?

GLOSSARY

anti-reflective coated with a film that reduces the strength of reflected light

barb hook-shaped part

carnivorous meat eating

coast land next to an ocean or sea

crustacean sea animal with an outer skeleton, such as a crab, lobster or shrimp

current movement of water in a river or an ocean

expedition journey with a goal, such as exploring or searching for something

fin body part that fish use to swim and steer in water

forensic using science to help investigate or solve crimes

gill body part on the side of a fish; fish use gills to breathe

habitat natural place and conditions in which a plant or animal lives

marine living in a body of water

microscope tool that makes very small things look large enough to be seen

mollusc animal with a soft body and no spine; a mollusc is usually protected by a hard shell

NASA US government agency that researches flight and space exploration

radiocarbon dating method of measuring the type of carbon in an object to determine how old it is

scavenger animal that feeds on whatever it can find

silt small particles of soil that settle at the bottom of a river, lake or ocean

vertebrate any animal that has a backbone; fish are vertebrates

volcano opening in Earth's surface that may send out hot lava, steam and ash

zooplankton small floating or weakly swimming organisms that drift with water currents

COMPREHENSION AND RESEARCH QUESTIONS

1. Hyperiid amphipods are scavengers. What does "scavenger" mean? Name another animal that is a scavenger.

2. Harp sponges are carnivores. Name another carnivorous sponge.

3. Explain the differences between brittle stars and starfish.

FIND OUT MORE

BOOKS
Deep Oceans (Earth's Last Frontiers), Ellen Labrecque (Raintree, 2015)

Ocean: A Children's Encyclopedia, John Woodward (DK Children, 2015)

Ocean Food Chains (Food Chains and Webs), Angela Royston (Raintree, 2014)

Oceans (Habitat Survival), Claire Llewellyn (Raintree, 2013)

WEBSITES
Find out more about coral reefs at:
www.dkfindout.com/uk/animals-and-nature/habitats-and-ecosystems/coral-reef

Learn more about the Cassini space mission at:
www.esa.int/esaKIDSen/SEM1U8WJD1E_OurUniverse_0.html

INDEX